Fun Facts about Oxygen

Chemistry for Kids

The Element Series

Children's Chemistry Books

BABY PROFESSOR

EDUCATION KIDS

Speedy Publishing LLC
40 E. Main St. #1156
Newark, DE 19711
www.speedypublishing.com

Oxygen is one of the most important elements as it is needed by most forms of live to survive on Earth. You may think of it as the air we breathe. It is known as the third most abundant element in our universe and the most abundant in your body. Read further to learn more about this element such as its characteristics, its uses, and how it was discovered.

Characteristics and Properties of Oxygen

Oxygen consists of 8 protons and 8 electrons. It can found at the top of column 16 of the periodic table.

8
O
Oxygen
15.9994

Water Molecules H_2O

Under usual conditions it forms a gas composed of molecules made of two oxygen atoms (O2). This is known as a diatomic gas. It its gaseous form it is odorless, colorless, and tasteless. Additionally, it exists as O3, the allotrope ozone. The ozone exists in an upper region of the atmosphere of the Earth, creating an ozone layer which protects us from the sun's harmful rays.

Even though we have this ozone layer, we should still wear sunscreen every day. In its pure state, it is very reactive and it can create compounds from several other elements. It dissolves in water quickly.

O₂
Oxygen

H2O Molecule

Oxidation is the process of combining it with different atoms to make compounds.

Electrolysis is the process of converting water to hydrogen and oxygen.

When concentrated, it promotes a quick combustion. This is why you see "No Smoking" signs around people that are using it for breathing.

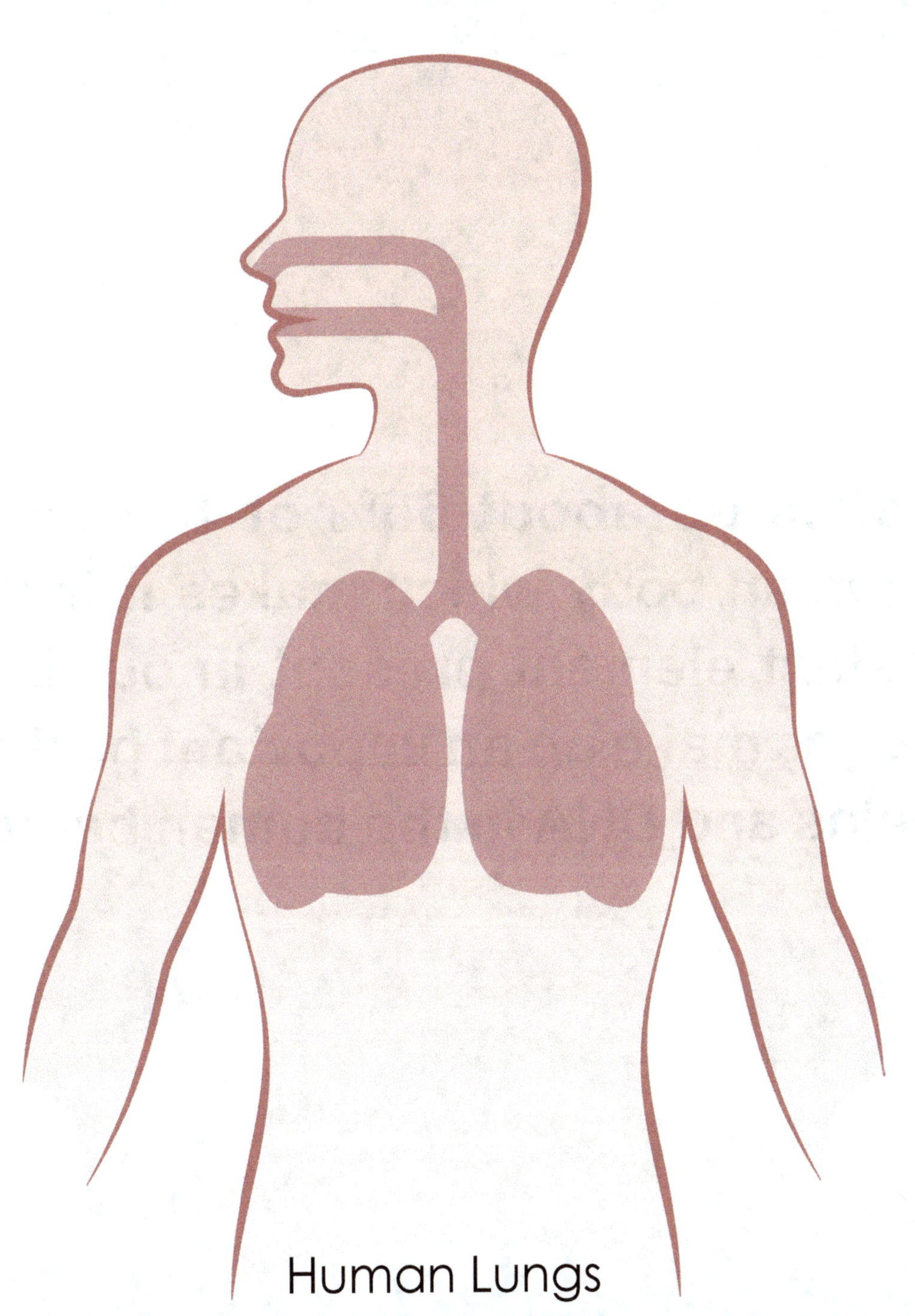
Human Lungs

It makes up about 65% of the mass of the human body which makes it the most abundant element present in our bodies. Its atoms make up an important part of the proteins and DNA in the human body.

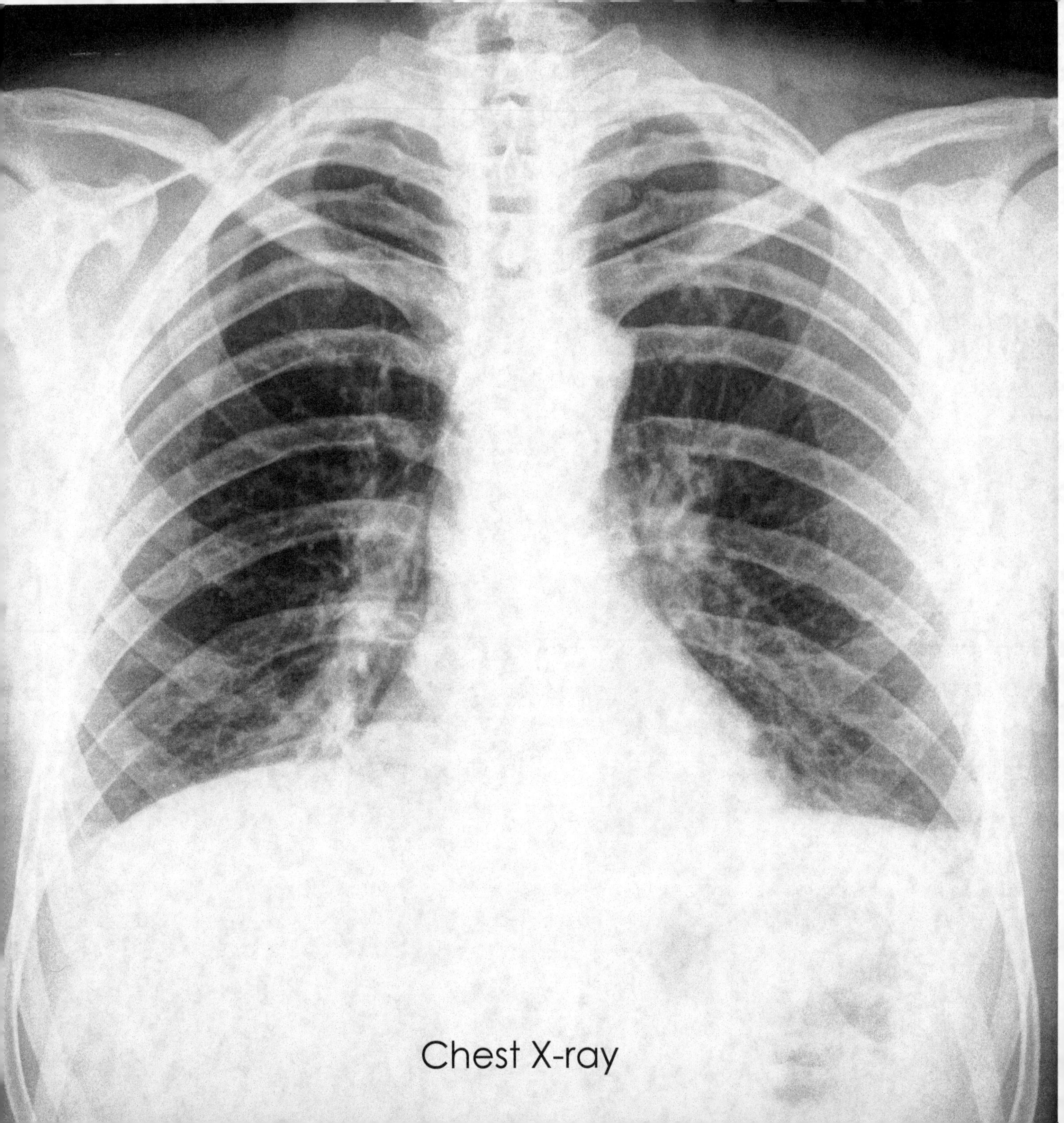

Chest X-ray

Oxygen Difluoride Molecular Structure

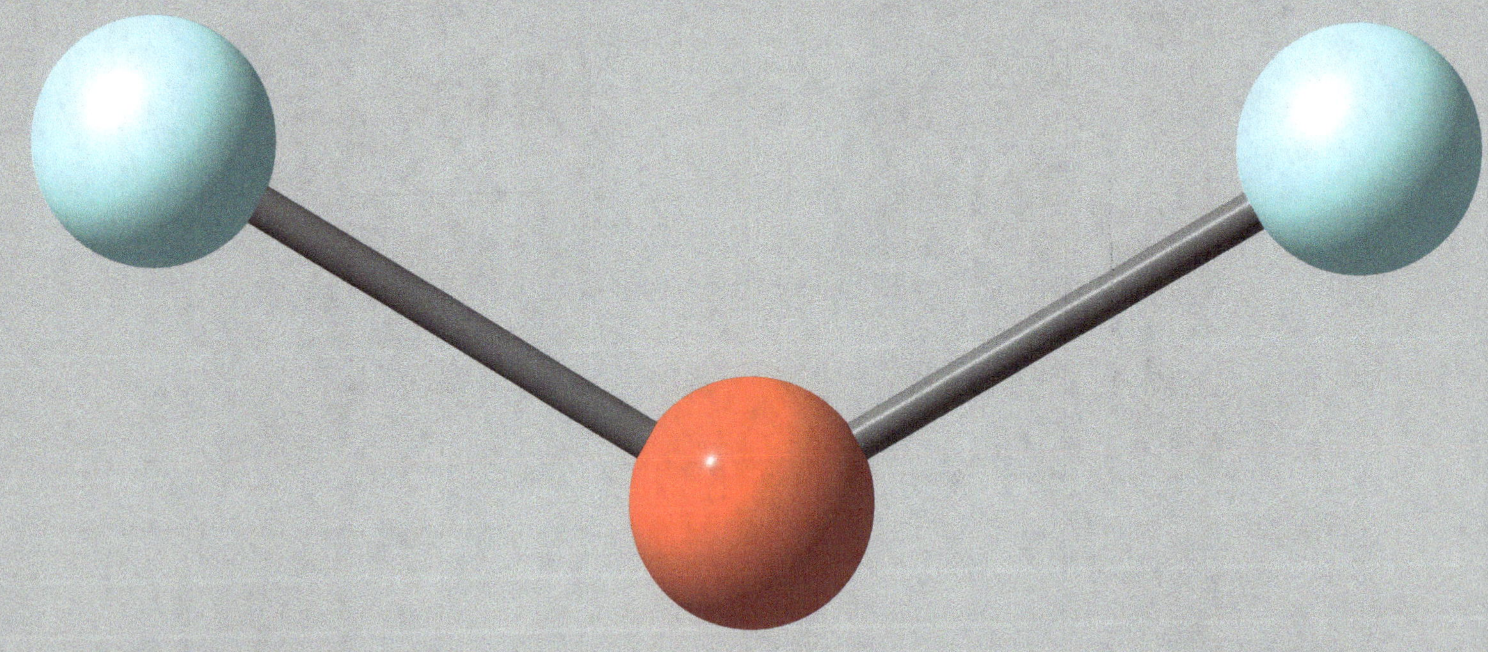

Oxygen Forms

Dioxygen is the common allotrope of its elemental form on Earth, O2. It is most commonly found in this form, including approximately 21% of the atmosphere of the Earth. Its bond length is 121 pm and has an energy bond of 48 kJ/mol. Oxygen is a colorless gas and has a boils at -183 degrees Celsius.

Singlet oxygen is the name used in the diamagnetic form of O2. Due to the unusual properties, it can persist for longer than an hour at room temperature, dependent upon its environment. Due to the difference of its electron shells, the chemical properties of singlet and triplet oxygen can vary. Singlet oxygen is what can damage sunlight on organic materials such as polymers.

Oxygen

View of Earth from space

Ozone is a triatomic molecule and contains three oxygen atoms. As an allotrope, it is much less stable that its diatomic allotrope. It is a pollutant in the air and can cause respiratory difficulties. However, it is beneficial in the upper layer of the atmosphere and can prevent damaging ultraviolet light reaching the surface of the Earth. There are many ways it can be used in consumer and industrial applications.

Tetraoxygen is suspected to have existed since early 1900s, then known as oxozone. It was then identified in 2001 at the University of Rome by a team organized by F. Cacace. O_4 is a molecule thought to be a solid phase which later was identified as O_8. This team felt that O_4 more than likely consisted of two O_2 molecules that looked similar to dumbbells, and held loosely together by forces induced by dipole dispersion.

Ozone Molecule Ball and Stick Model

Liquid water
Hydrogen bonds

Solid Oxygen consists of 6 distinct phases. One appears as a cluster of dark-red O8. When it is exposed to 96 GPa pressure, it appears metallic, similar to hydrogen, it then becomes heavier such as chalcogens, similar to polonium and tellurium, both that show a substantial metallic character. When it occurs in temperatures that are very low, it also becomes a superconductor.

Liquid oxygen is also known as LOX, or Lox in the gas, submarine, and aerospace industries. It is light blue in color and strongly paramagnetic and can suspend among poles of a powerful horseshoe magnet. Its density is 1.141 g/cm3 and its freezing point is 50.5K which makes is a cryogenic. It is classified as an industrial gas and widely used for medical and industrial purposes. It is obtained from the oxygen naturally found in the air by fractional distillation. It has a ratio expansion of 861.1 when at 68 degrees Fahrenheit (20 degrees Celsius and is used as breathing oxygen in military and commercial aircraft.

OXIDIZING
GAS
2
OXYGEN
UN 1072
NET WEIGHT
20 KG
FOR INDUSTRIAL USE ONLY

OXIDIZING
GAS
2
OXYGEN
UN 1072
NET WEIGHT
25 KG
FOR INDUSTRIAL USE ONLY

OXIDIZING
GAS
2
OXYGEN
UN 1072
NET WEIGHT
10 KG
FOR INDUSTRIAL USE ONLY

OXIDIZING
GAS
2
OXYGEN
UN 1072
NET WEIGHT
8 KG

OXIDIZING
GAS
2
OXYGEN
UN 1072
NET WEIGHT
6 KG

Where can it be found on Earth?

It is all around us. It is considered to be one of the most significant element on this planet. Earth is the only planet in our solar system that contains a high percentage of it. Approximately 21% of our atmosphere and 50% of the Earth's crust mass is made up of it. Water is made using one atom of it (H_2O). It is also considered a substantial element of life on this planet.

The Oxygen Cycle

This cycle is a biogeochemical and describes how it moves between its main three reservoirs, including the atmosphere, the content of biological matter in our biosphere, which is the global sum of all of the ecosystems, and lithosphere, the Earth's crust.

The Oxygen Cycle

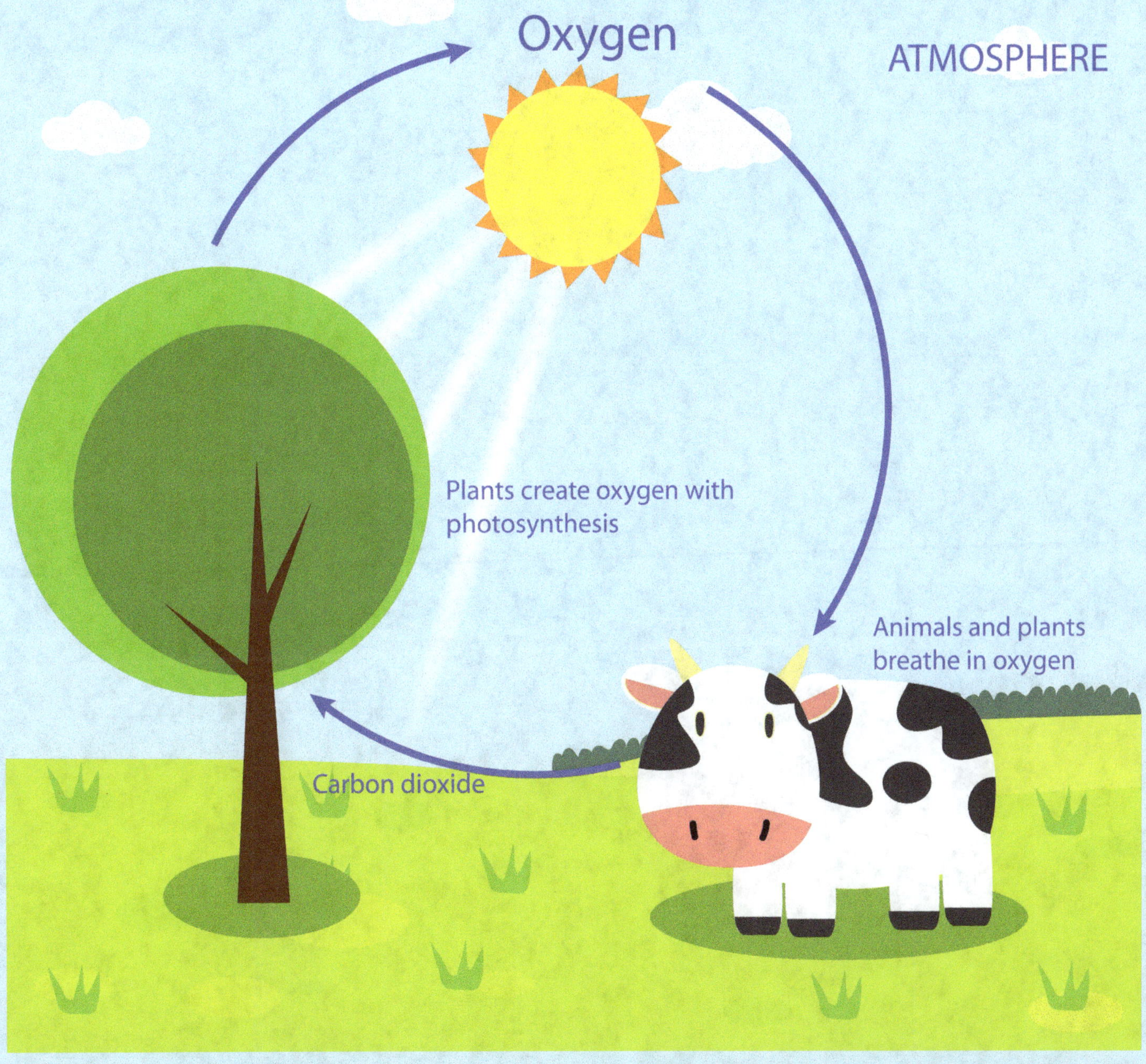

Failures in this cycle can result in development of hypoxic zones. The main factor of this cycle is photosynthesis, which results in our atmosphere and life.

How do we use it today?

It is used by plants and animals in their breathing (respiration) process. Photosynthesis produces the oxygen found in our atmosphere. There would be only a small amount of it in the air without plants.

Two Oxygen Cylinders

Have you seen tanks filled with oxygen? These are used in the medical field for people that have difficulty breathing. They are also used by scuba divers and astronauts for breathing.

In industry, it is used for steel manufacturing. It is also used to make new compounds similar to plastics and generating a hot flame as is used in welding. Rocket Fuel is made when liquid oxygen is mixed with liquid hydrogen.

REFILL
1000 2000
3000
PSI
OXYGEN
USE NO OIL
MADE IN U.S.A.

How was it discovered?

One of the first experiments regarding the reaction between air and combustion was done by Philo of Byzantium, a 2nd century Greek writer. In Pneumatica, Philo detected when inverting a container over a candle that is burning and surrounding it with water would result in some of the water rising. He incorrectly deduced that some of the air was converted into fire and had the ability to escape amid the pores of the glass. Centuries later Leonardo da Vinci expanded on Philo's work by noting that a portion of it is consumed throughout respiration and combustion.

In 1772, it was first discovered by a Swedish chemist named C. W. Steele. He referred to this gas as "fire air" since it was required to burn fire. He did not issue his findings immediately and the element was then discovered in 1774 by Joseph Priestley.

Medical Oxygen Concentrator

Scuba diving tanks

Its name stems from the Greek word "oxygenes" meaning "acid producer". Early chemists thought it was used for all acids. It was named this since early chemists felt that it was required for all acids.

Isotopes

Isotopes consist of variants of an element that differ in their number of neutrons.

8
O
Oxygen
15.9994

oxygen
O
8

Each isotope of a particular element contains equal proton numbers in each of their atoms. Isotope stems from the Greek term isos (equal) combined with topos (place), which means same place. Hence, the meaning different isotopes of a particular element reside on the periodic table in the same position.

Oxygen consists of three stable isotopes, O-16, O-17, and O-18. Its relative atomic mass is 15.9994(3). More than 99% of stable oxygen consists of isotope oxygen-16. Its isotopes are known to range in their mass from 12 to 24.

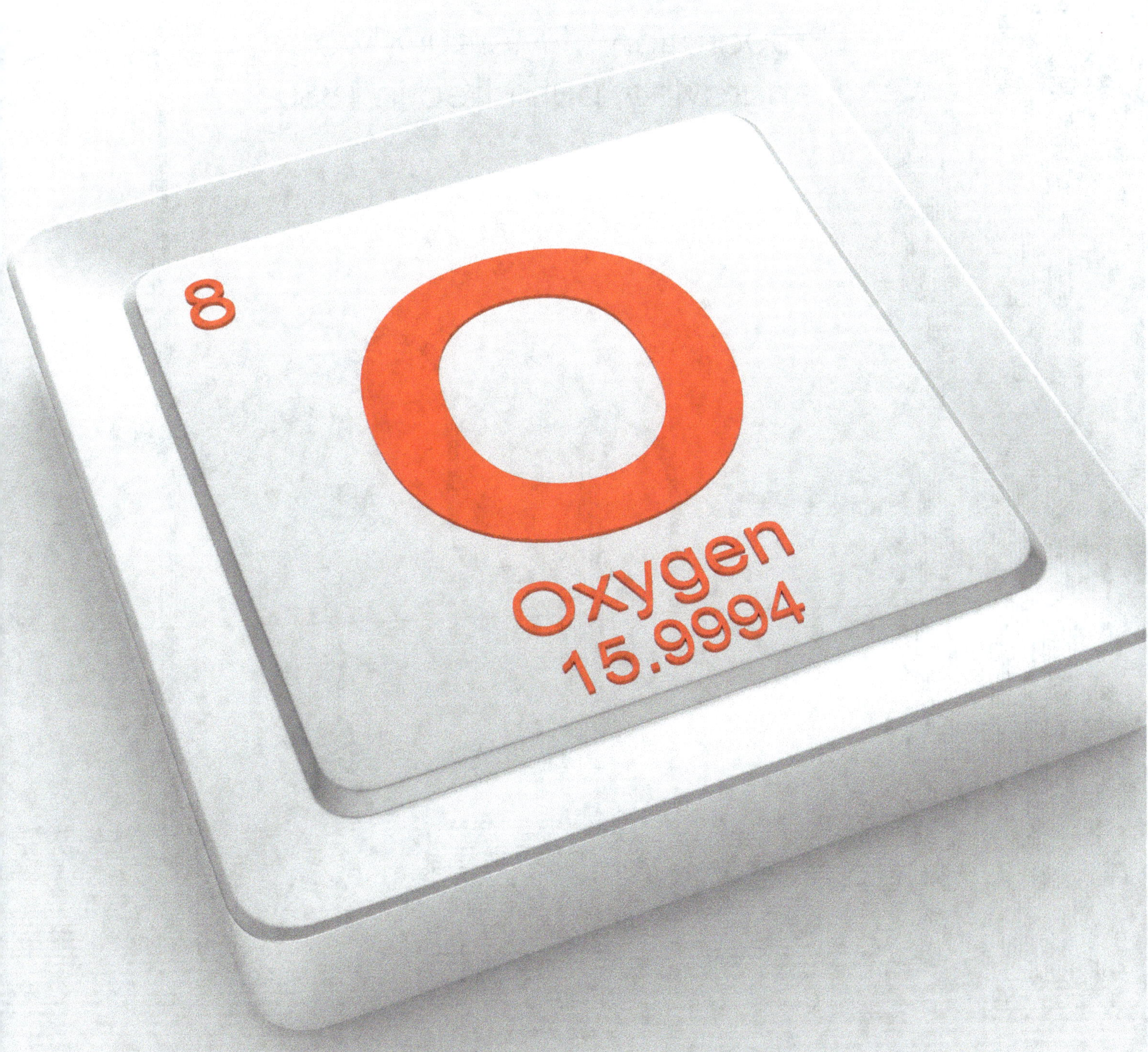
8
Oxygen
15.9994

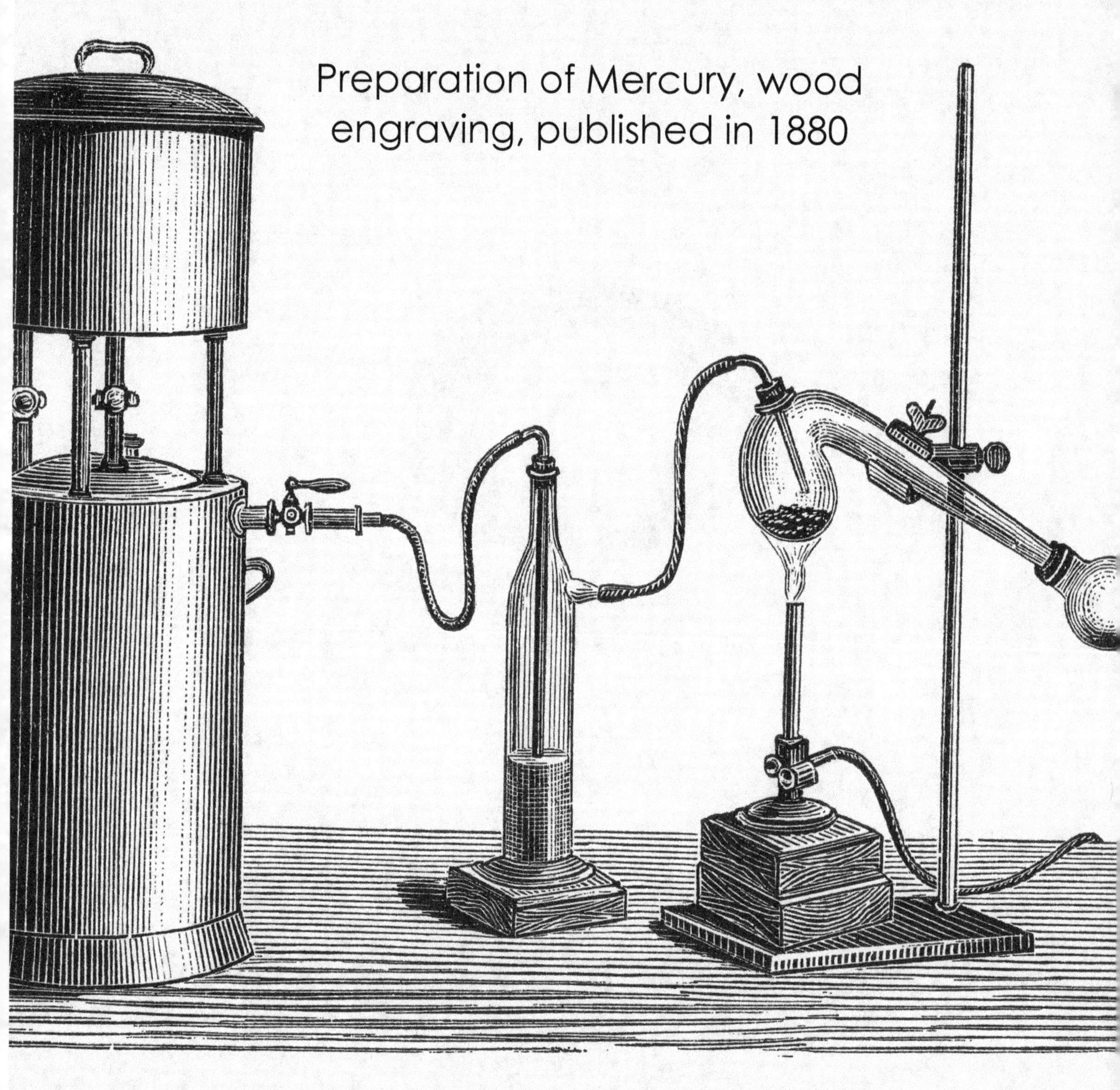

Preparation of Mercury, wood
engraving, published in 1880

Toxicity

Oxygen toxicity results when we breathe molecular oxygen at partial elevated pressures. It is also referred to as oxygen intoxication, oxygen poisoning, and toxicity syndrome. The central nervous system toxicity was known as the Paul Bert effect and the pulmonary condition was known as the Lorrain Smith effect. More severe toxicity can result in damage to cells, and even death, with the central nervous system and eyes being most affected. It is also a major issue with scuba divers, people using a high concentration, in particular, premature babies, the people using hyperbaric oxygen therapy.

Periodic Table of Elements

There is so much more to learn about this element as well as the many other elements. You may want to research the periodic table of elements which lists all the elements including their atomic structure. In 1869, a Russian chemist named Dmitri Mendeleev came up with this table. With the use of this table, he had the ability to predict properties of elements prior to them being discovered.

PERIODIC TABLE OF THE ELEMENTS

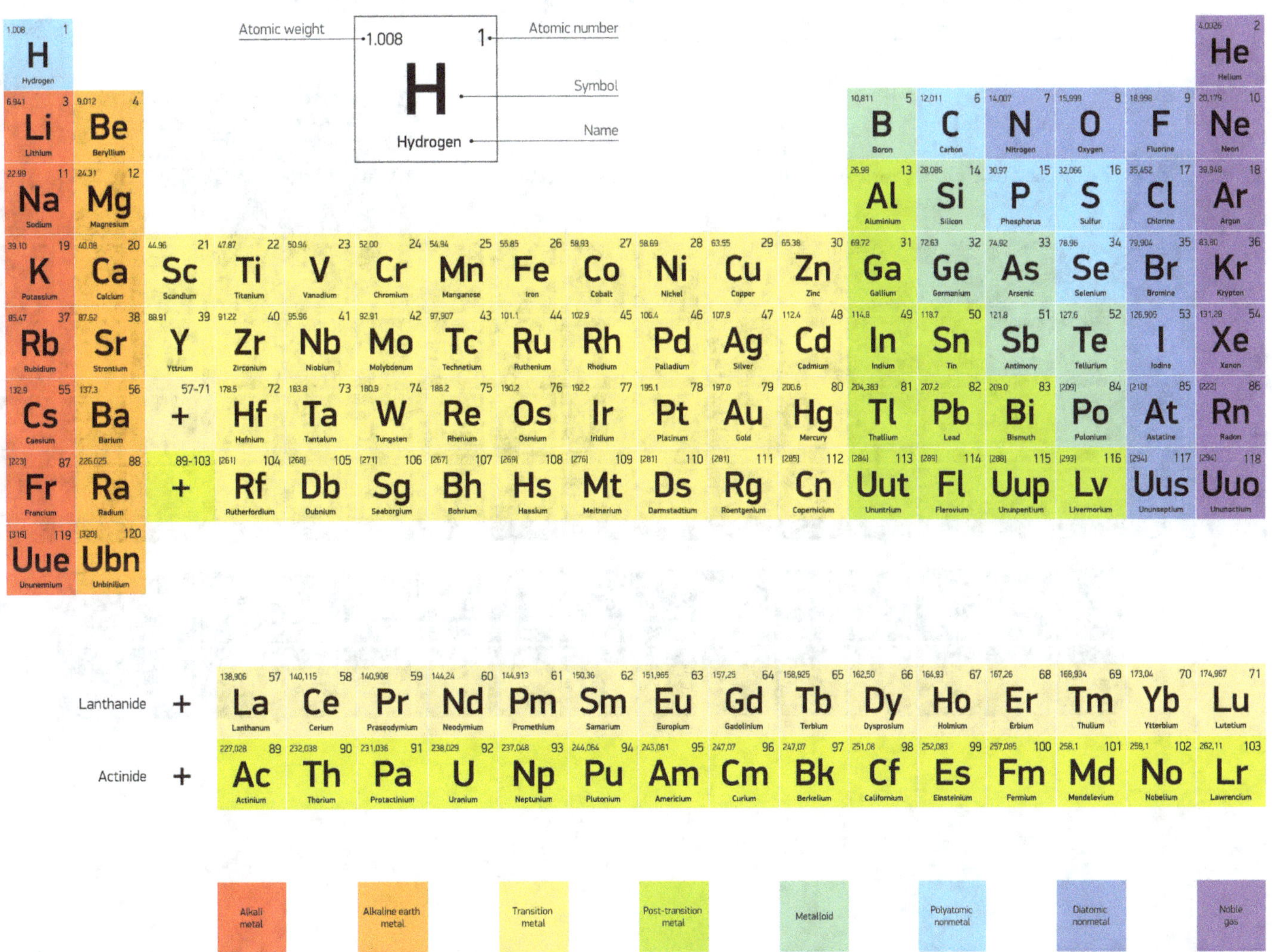

PERIODIC TABLE OF THE ELEMENTS

Non-metal
Alkali metal
Alkaline earth metal
Transition metal

Metal
Metalloid
Halogen

Noble gas
Lanthanide
Actinide

1 H HYDROGEN 1.0079																	2 He HELIUM 4.0026
3 Li LITHIUM 6.941	4 Be BERYLLIUM 9.0122											5 B BORON 10.811	6 C CARBON 12.011	7 N NITROGEN 14.007	8 O OXYGEN 15.999	9 F FLUORINE 18.998	10 Ne NEON 20.1797
11 Na SODIUM 22.989	12 Mg MAGNESIUM 24.305											13 Al ALUMINIUM 26.981	14 Si SILICON 28.085	15 P PHOSPHORUS 30.974	16 S SULFUR 32.066	17 Cl CHLORINE 35.453	18 Ar ARGON 39.948
19 K POTASSIUM 39.098	20 Ca CALCIUM 40.078	21 Sc SCANDIUM 44.955	22 Ti TITANIUM 47.867	23 V VANADIUM 50.9415	24 Cr CHROMIUM 51.9961	25 Mn MANGANESE 54.938	26 Fe IRON 55.845	27 Co COBALT 58.933	28 Ni NICKEL 58.6934	29 Cu COPPER 63.546	30 Zn ZINC 65.38	31 Ga GALLIUM 69.723	32 Ge GERMANIUM 72.63	33 As ARSENIC 74.921	34 Se SELENIUM 78.971	35 Br BROMINE 79.904	36 Kr KRYPTON 83.798
37 Rb RUBIDIUM 85.467	38 Sr STRONTIUM 87.62	39 Y YTTRIUM 88.9058	40 Zr ZICRONIUM 91.224	41 Nb NIOBIUM 92.9063	42 Mo MOLYBDENUM 95.95	43 Tc TECHNETIUM (98)	44 Ru RUTHENIUM 101.07	45 Rh RHODIUM 102.90	46 Pd PALLADIUM 106.42	47 Ag SILVER 107.8682	48 Cd CADMIUM 112.414	49 In INDIUM 114.818	50 Sn TIN 118.710	51 Sb ANTIMONY 121.760	52 Te TELLURIUM 127.60	53 I IODINE 126.90	54 Xe XENON 131.293
55 Cs CAESIUM 132.905	56 Ba BARIUM 137.327	57-71	72 Hf HAFNIUM 178.49	73 Ta TANTALUM 180.94	74 W TUNGSTEN 183.84	75 Re RHENIUM 186.207	76 Os OSMIUM 190.23	77 Ir IRIDIUM 192.217	78 Pt PLATINUM 195.084	79 Au GOLD 196.96	80 Hg MERCURY 200.59	81 Tl THALLIUM 204.38	82 Pb LEAD 207.2	83 Bi BISMUTH 208.98	84 Po POLONIUM (209)	85 At ASTATINE (210)	86 Rn RADON (222)
87 Fr FRANCIUM (223)	88 Ra RADIUM (226)	89-103	104 Rf RUTHERFORDIUM (267)	105 Db DUBNIUM (268)	106 Sg SEABORGIUM (271)	107 Bh BOHRIUM (272)	108 Hs HASSIUM (270)	109 Mt MEITNERIUM (276)	110 Ds DARMSTADTIUM (281)	111 Rg ROENTGENIUM (280)	112 Cn COPERNICIUM (285)	113 Uut UNUNTRIUM (284)	114 Fl FLEROVIUM (289)	115 Uup UNUNPENTIUM (288)	116 Lv LIVERMORIUM (293)	117 Uus UNUNSEPTIUM (294)	118 Uuo UNUNOCTIUM (294)

*	57 La LANTHANUM 138.90	58 Ce CERIUM 140.116	59 Pr PRASEODYMIUM 140.90	60 Nd NEODYMIUM 144.242	61 Pm PROMETHIUM (145)	62 Sm SAMARIUM 150.36	63 Eu EUROPIUM 151.964	64 Gd GADOLINIUM 157.25	65 Tb TERIBIUM 158.92	66 Dy DYSPROSIUM 162.500	67 Ho HOLMIUM 164.93	68 Er ERBIUM 167.259	69 Tm THULIUM 168.93	70 Yb YTTERBIUM 173.054	71 Lu LUTETIUM 174.9668
**	89 Ac ACTINIUM (227)	90 Th THORIUM 232.0377	90 Pa PROTACTINIUM 231.03	92 U URANIUM 238.02	93 Np NEPTUNIUM (237)	94 Pu PLUTONIUM (244)	95 Am AMERICIUM (243)	96 Cm CURIUM (247)	97 Bk BERKELIUM (247)	98 Cf CALIFORNIUM (251)	99 Es EINSTEINIUM (252)	100 Fm FERMIUM (257)	101 Md MENDELEVIUM (258)	102 No NOBELIUM (259)	103 Lr LAWRENCIUM (262)

The table is divided into groups in order to assist chemists working with these elements to learn and product how an element may behave or react in certain situations.

This table lists the name and abbreviation for each element. You may find some abbreviations easy to remember, such as H which is the abbreviation for hydrogen but some like iron (Fe) and gold (Au) are a somewhat more difficult to remember. In the instance of gold, "Au" originates from "aurum", which is the Latin word for gold.

THE PERIODIC TABLE OF ELEMENTS

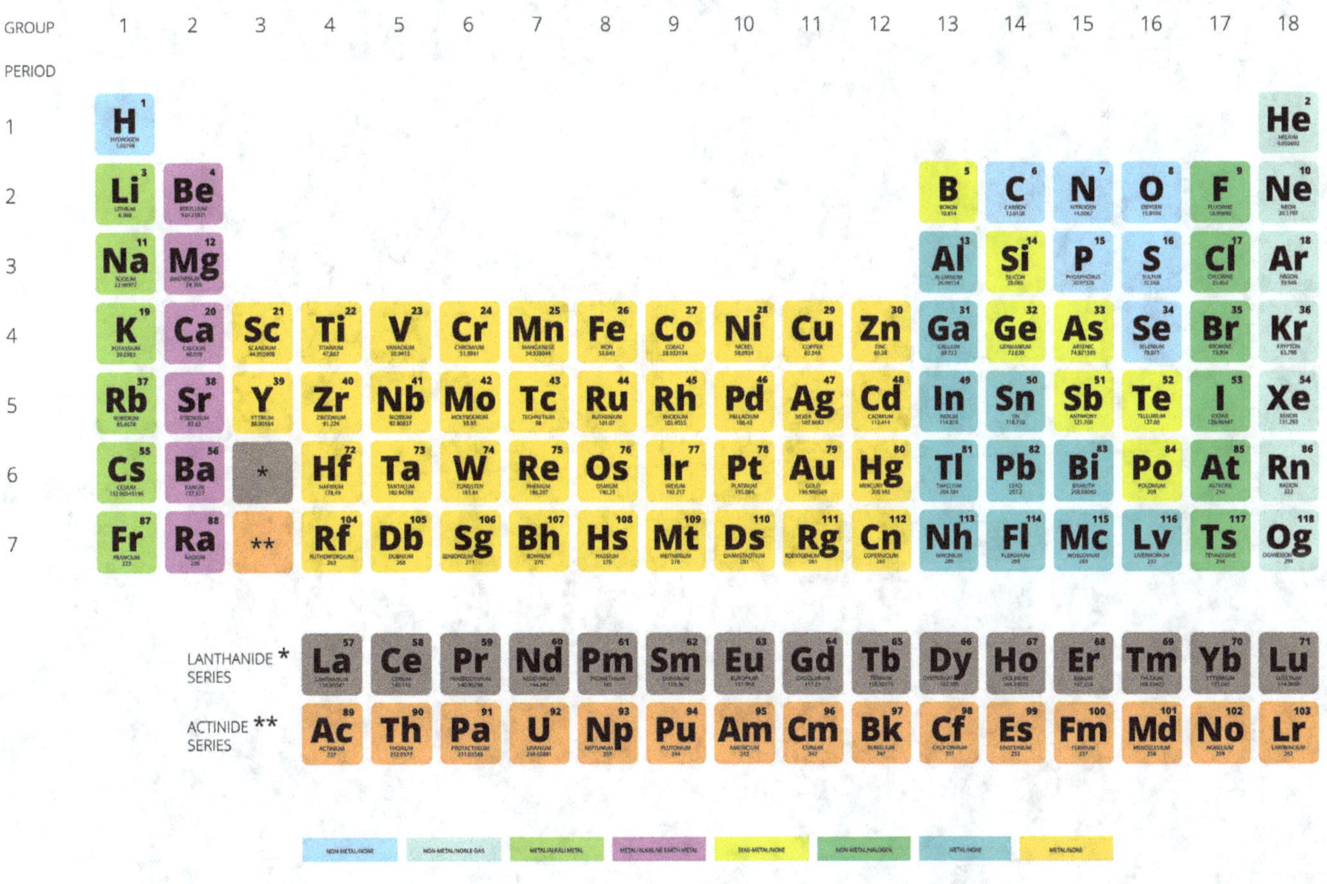

You can learn more by researching on the internet or by reaching out to your teachers, parents, and friends for additional information.

Visit
BABY PROFESSOR
EDUCATION KIDS
www.BabyProfessorBooks.com
to download Free Baby Professor eBooks
and view our catalog of new and exciting
Children's Books